Sticks and Bricks and Bits of Stone

Scoular Anderson

Contents

CAMBRIDGE
UNIVERSITY PRESS

UCL
Institute of Education

Thousands of years of building

People have been making buildings for thousands and thousands of years. Buildings are the biggest man-made things on Earth.

The first buildings were made of wooden poles covered with animal skins.

When people learned to build with bricks or stone they had to learn how to move heavy materials.

The Romans invented the arch which added strength to buildings. This meant that buildings could get much bigger.

People became very skilful at using all sorts of stuff – wood, reeds, bamboo, leaves, stone, glass – to make and decorate their buildings.

Some buildings are
simple and beautiful.
Some are amazingly grand.

The Temple of Angkor Wat in Cambodia is almost 1,000 years old. It is one of the biggest buildings in the world. ↘

pattern made by ↑ a simple roof of palm leaves

Build a wall

Many buildings are just walls. People built walls to **protect** their country from enemies.

The biggest wall is known as the Great Wall of China. It was built many hundreds of years ago and is 8,850 kilometres long.

There were **watchtowers** along its length.

The Great Wall of Zimbabwe in Africa surrounded a city of about 18,000 people. It was begun nearly 1,000 years ago and took nearly 300 years to complete.

In fact, there were two walls, one inside the other, built in a circle. →

The Romans built Hadrian's Wall in the north of England. It stretches from coast to coast for 117 kilometres.

The Romans could keep an eye on people as they came through the wall.

ruined fort

Get some mud

Mud is one of the oldest building materials.
Mud bricks are made from a mixture of mud, sand
and water. Straw is mixed in to make the bricks stronger.

The mud mixture is packed into wooden boxes. Then it is
turned out and left in the sun to dry and get hard.

The Great Mosque of Djenné
in Mali, Africa, is the biggest
mud building in
the world.

Shibam in Yemen is a town of tall mud brick houses. Some of these are eleven **storeys** high.

For safety reasons, there are no windows near the ground.

a strong door →

Mud brick buildings are covered in a layer of mud to protect them from the weather.

The **minaret** of the Great Mosque at Samarra, Iraq, is over 1,000 years old. You go around and around a **spiral ramp** to the top.

More bricks

As time went on, people used clay or concrete bricks. They are harder than mud bricks and can be used for bigger buildings.

Bricks are much smaller than blocks of stone, so it is easier to build unusual shapes with them.

Saint Basil's Cathedral in Moscow, Russia, is built of brick and it has fantastic shaped domes and towers. →

This is a stupa. It is a shrine built in the shape of a **dome**.
Some stupas are the oldest and
biggest brick buildings in the world.

The Jetavana Stupa in Sri Lanka contains about 93 million bricks and is 1,700 years old.

If bricks are put around a steel framework, they can be built into very high buildings.

The Chrysler Building in New York is the tallest brick building in the world.

Timber

Wood which has been cut and prepared for building is called timber. Timber has been used to make buildings for thousands of years. It is **flexible**, strong and easily carved.

Saint George's Cathedral in Guyana, South America, is the biggest wooden church in the world.

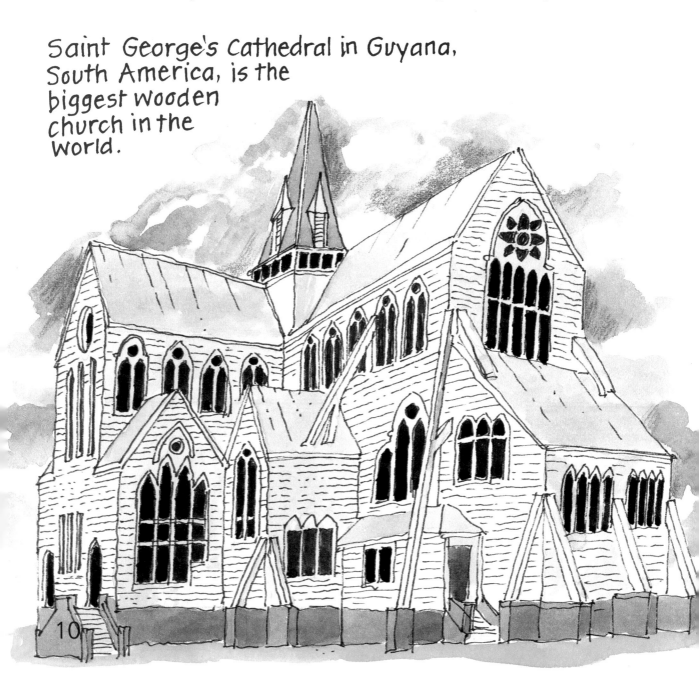

Fire can be a great danger to wooden buildings. Himeji Castle in Japan has been rebuilt many times and has survived earthquakes and bombs.

Heddal church in Norway was built nearly 800 years ago and is made entirely of wood, including the roof.

A legend says the church was built in three days by a troll. (A wicked giant!)

Sandstone and granite

Sandstone is a soft rock, so it can be cut and carved quite easily. It is made up of grains of sand which were squeezed together millions of years ago.

Granite is a very hard rock. It has dark speckles in it and can be lots of different colours – pink, brown, blue, black and grey.

The huge **amphitheatre** at El Djem, Tunisia was built out of sandstone by the Romans. Today it is in ruins.

35,000 people could sit down inside to watch gladiator fights.

The Palace of the Winds is in Jaipur, India. It is made of pink and red sandstone and it has 953 windows.

The windows of the palace have a lattice design to allow air to flow in and cool the rooms. ←

This is the tower of Marischal College, Aberdeen, one of the biggest granite buildings in the world. ↗

Aberdeen in Scotland is called 'the Granite City' because most of its buildings are made of granite.

Limestone and coral

Limestone is made up of the shells and skeletons of sea creatures which fell to the bottom of the oceans. Over millions of years they were squeezed together to make a pale-coloured rock.

Saint Paul's Cathedral in London is built of limestone from the south coast of England.

The Romans built aqueducts to bring water to their cities. Aqueducts carried water over great distances.

The aqueduct at Nîmes, France, crosses the River Gard. It is 50 kilometres long and made of limestone blocks.

14

Coral is formed underwater by small sea creatures.
These creatures have a hard outer shell and over millions
of years their shells turn into huge masses called reefs.
Coral can be cut into blocks to make buildings.

Lamu, in Kenya, East Africa,
has buildings of coral. It is
the country's oldest town.

River Gard

Marble and mosaic

Marble is a **popular** stone for building because it can be polished so that it sparkles in the light. It comes in many colours including black, pink, green and red, often with swirling patterns.

The Taj Mahal at Agra, India, was built of white marble by Emperor Shah Jahan in memory of his wife, Mumtaz Mahal.

The walls of the cathedral in Florence, Italy, are decorated with white, green and red marble.

← the dome of the cathedral

A mosaic is made up of tiny bits of marble, stone or glass pressed into wet concrete.

This strange building in Barcelona, Spain, is covered in mosaics.

17

Going up

All through history, people have built amazingly tall and grand buildings. Great skills were needed for this.

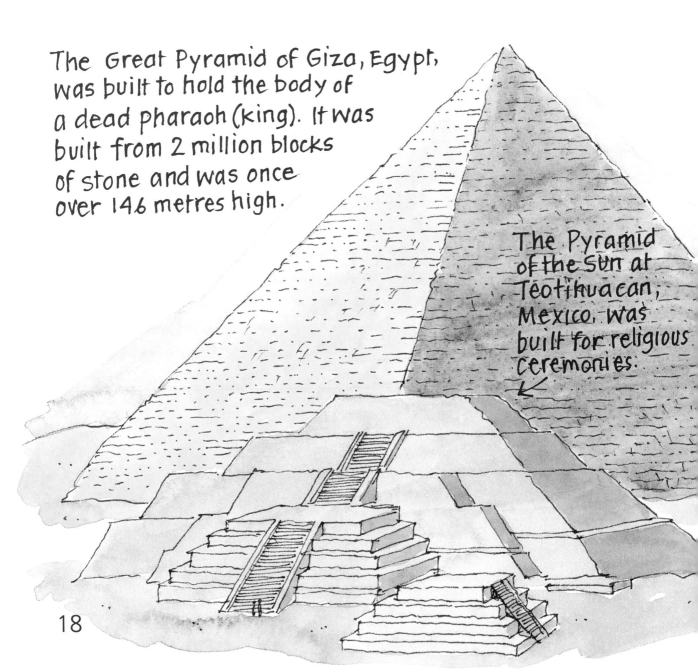

The Great Pyramid of Giza, Egypt, was built to hold the body of a dead pharaoh (king). It was built from 2 million blocks of stone and was once over 146 metres high.

The Pyramid of the Sun at Teotihuacan, Mexico, was built for religious ceremonies.

Some of the tallest buildings
have such thin and delicate
stonework that they look as if
they are made of lace or paper.

Ulm Minster, Germany,
is the tallest church in
the world. It is more
than 161 metres high.

Build on water

Some people don't let water put them off building things. It is possible to build houses on piles. Piles are wooden poles. The city of Venice, Italy, is built on water. Piles were driven into the **shallow** sea between tiny islands and houses were built on top.

People travel around Venice by boat.

Underneath the city of Istanbul, Turkey, there is a huge stone water tank called the Basilica Cistern. The roof is held up by 336 marble columns.

The stones of the Cistern were stolen from other places so that explains the head of a giant statue at the foot of a column!

Houses can be built on man-made islands. The houses and islands are both made from reeds tied together in large bundles.

The Arab al-Ahwar (Marsh Arabs) of Iraq live in houses on floating islands called kibasha.

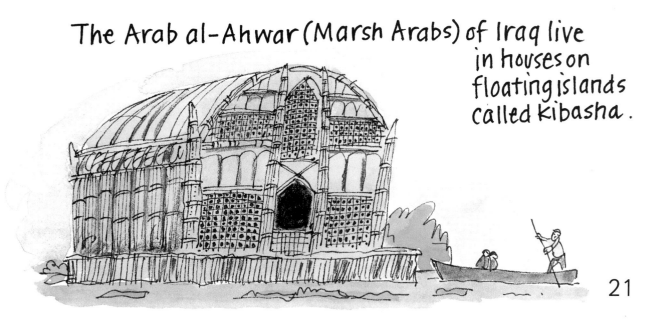

Add decoration

People like decorating their buildings with patterns or pictures. Sometimes they just paint the walls of their houses. Sometimes they use mud or **plaster** to make **raised** patterns.

raised patterns on buildings in Ghana, West Africa

In Burkina Faso, Africa, they paint chevrons, squares and diamonds on their houses.

The roofs of the Grand Palace in Bangkok, Thailand are covered in shining gold.

22

There are buildings all over the world decorated with carved wood.

Parts of this house in Indonesia have patterns of flowers.

When iron is heated until it melts it can be poured into **moulds**. It is called cast iron and can be used to decorate buildings.

house in Australia, decorated with cast iron

23

Building bridges

People have always wanted to move around. Long ago they used simple paths through the countryside. Slowly the paths got bigger and better and people began to find ways of crossing difficult **barriers**, like rivers.

The Qhapaq Nan roads were built around 400 years ago. They stretch 30,000 kilometres from one end of South America to the other.

Modern road bridges are made of concrete. Steel **cables** hold up the road platform.

The Millau motorway bridge in France is the tallest bridge in the world.

Some bridges are made of steel. They are designed in a special way so they don't **collapse** in the middle. Bridges that cross rivers have to be high enough to let ships go underneath.

The Forth Rail Bridge in Scotland took 7 years to build.

All shapes and sizes

Concrete has been used in buildings for thousands of years. Glass windows have been used in buildings for around 800 years. A hundred years ago, people learned to use steel, glass and concrete to build in new and exciting ways. Buildings didn't have to be built in the old ways any more. They could be any shape!

The Sydney Opera House, Australia, looks like the sails of yachts. The curved roofs are covered in over a million concrete tiles.

The Heydar Aliyev Centre in Azerbaijan swirls around like flowing water.

People have always tried to outdo each other by building taller and taller. The Eiffel Tower in Paris, France, was the tallest building for 41 years. Today, the Burj Khalifa is the tallest building in the world.

Finished in 2010, the Burj Khalifa, Dubai, has 163 floors and is 829 metres high. →

Built in 1889, the Eiffel Tower is the most visited building on earth. ↓

Where the buildings are

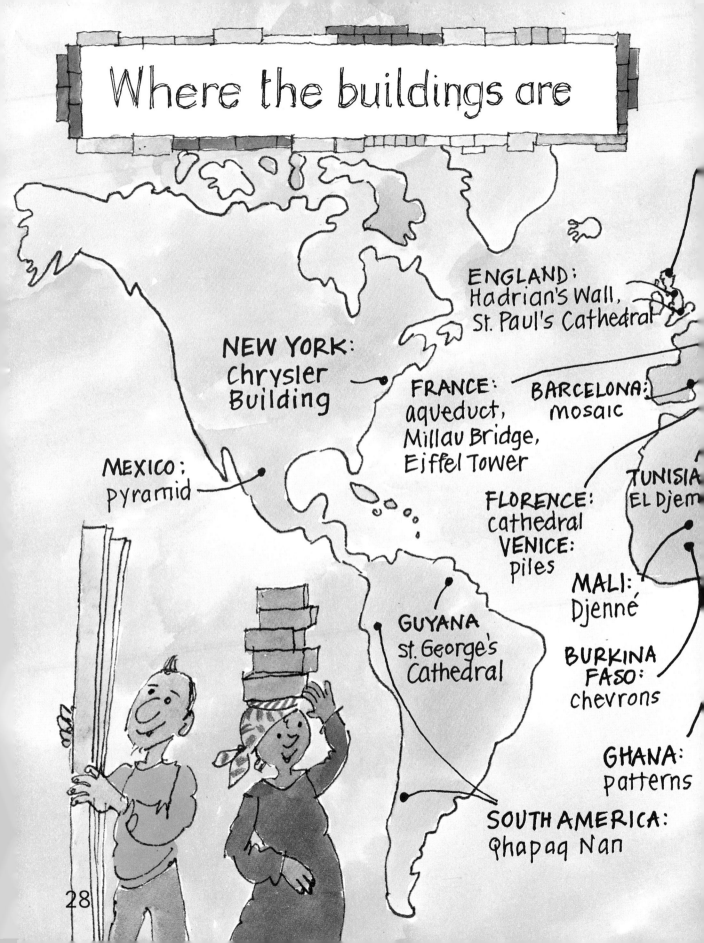

ENGLAND:
Hadrian's Wall,
St. Paul's Cathedral

NEW YORK:
Chrysler
Building

FRANCE:
aqueduct,
Millau Bridge,
Eiffel Tower

BARCELONA:
mosaic

MEXICO:
pyramid

TUNISIA
El Djem

FLORENCE:
cathedral
VENICE:
piles

MALI:
Djenné

GUYANA
St. George's
Cathedral

BURKINA
FASO:
chevrons

GHANA:
patterns

SOUTH AMERICA:
Qhapaq Nan

SCOTLAND:
Forth Rail Bridge
Tower, Marischal College

NORWAY: Heddal Church

GERMANY: Ulm Minster

MOSCOW: St. Basil's Cathedral

TURKEY: cistern

AZERBAIJAN: Aliyev Centre

IRAQ: kibasha
Samarra

DUBAI:
Burj Khalifa

CHINA:
Great
Wall

JAPAN
Himeji
Castle

CAMBODIA:
Temple of
Angkor Wat

EGYPT
pyramid

YEMEN
mud bricks

INDIA:
Palace
of the
Winds,
Taj Mahal

KENYA
Lamu

SRI LANKA:
stupa

INDONESIA:
painted wood

ZIMBABWE:
Great Wall

AUSTRALIA:
cast iron,
Sydney Opera House

Glossary

amphitheatre open-air place for entertainment and sports, used by the Romans

barriers things which stop a person from moving forwards

cables thick, strong wires

collapse fall to pieces

dome part of a building shaped like half a ball

flexible easily made into shapes

lattice open framework made of wood or stone

minaret tower of a mosque

moulds hollow containers used to make a shape

plaster building material which gives walls a smooth surface

popular liked by a lot of people

protect look after and keep safe

raised sticking out from the background

ruined fallen down

shallow water that is not deep

spiral ramp walkway going around and around to the top of a building

storeys floors of a building

watchtowers towers used by soldiers to keep watch over an area

Index

Sticks and Bricks and Bits of Stone · Scoular Anderson

Teaching notes written by Sue Bodman and Glen Franklin

Using this book

Developing reading comprehension

This illustrated non-fiction text explores the history of building. It is a companion text to Ships and Boats and Things that Float (Purple Band) which children may have read earlier in the Cambridge Reading Adventure Series. Non-fiction features include maps and a detailed glossary as well as many labels and captions which add specific information to that featured in the main body of the text.

Grammar and sentence structure

- Longer sentence structures containing two or more ideas and punctuated using commas.

- Adjectives and adverbial phrases are used to create effect or provide emphasis: 'fantastic shaped domes'; 'the biggest wooden church in the world'.

Word meaning and spelling

- Subject-specific vocabulary is supported by the glossary. Labels and captions provide additional information to support meaning.

Curriculum links

History – The book could be used in conjunction with studies of particular historical periods, alongside other non-fiction texts and websites.

Art – Children can experiment with different building materials to design and create their own house – what features would they really like to include?

Learning outcomes

Children can:

- search for and find information in texts more flexibly

- sustain interest in longer, more complex texts

- express opinions, considering authorial intent and interpretation.

A guided reading lesson

Book Introduction

Please note: This text starts by exploring the early history of buildings, and then goes on to investigate a range of building materials and styles. It is a book that can be revisited over two or three guided reading sessions. These lesson notes cover pages 2–10, with follow-up activities that lead into the next guided reading lesson.

If the children have read Ships and Boats and Things that Float (Purple band), revisit that text as an introduction, recalling how the author presents the information, and how the content is structured.

Orientation

Give a copy of the book to each child. Read the title and the blurb together. Ask: Can you tell me what you think this book is going to be about? Establish that the book is non-fiction, although unusually it is illustrated rather than using photographs.

Preparation

Ask the children to skim the contents page (page 1): Were there any words in the contents page that you didn't understand? (e.g. 'mosaic'). How will we find out? Prompt for a variety of ways this could be done: go to the chapter, look at the captions, use of the index. Note that the word 'mosaic' is not in the glossary – discuss why not with the children (as it is fully explained in the main text).

Choose a complex sentence which uses adjectives or an adjectival phrase, such as 'The first buildings were made of wooden poles covered with animal skins.' on page 2. Ensure the children are able to track meaning across this long sentence and can retell the intended message.

Set a purpose for reading by preparing some questions on cards based on the text, for example: 'Why was the Roman arch so important?'; 'Why did people build walls?' Say: We are going to reading this book several times